Why is plastic bad?

Written by Susannah Reed

Illustrated by Abdi

Collins

Who and what is in this book?

Listen and say

Dad

Matt

straw

plastic bottle

Download the audio at www.collins.co.uk/839682

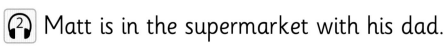 Matt is in the supermarket with his dad.

Matt says, "Can I have some water, please?"

Dad says, "Where is *your* water bottle, Matt?"

4

"It's at home," says Matt. "Can I have this bottle?"

"No," says Dad. "That's a plastic bottle. Plastic is bad."

"Why is plastic bad?" asks Matt.

Look at this picture. The table and chairs are plastic. The plates, bowls and cups are plastic. And the flowers are plastic, too!

You can buy plastic bottles, plastic bags, plastic toys, and plastic fruit and vegetables. You can buy plastic shoes, too.

Plastic is in a lot of things. Why is this bad?

After people use plastic things, they often throw them away. Then the plastic is rubbish.

Plastic rubbish is in our towns, parks and rivers. It's on our beaches and in our seas. In some places, there are mountains of rubbish.

Plastic rubbish is in the ground and in the sea for years. Some plastic in the sea is 60 years old! These fish are eating plastic rubbish. Plastic is not good food for fish.

What can we do? We can think about
the four R's: Refuse, Reduce, Reuse and
Recycle plastic.

Refuse! Always say "No" to plastic.

Don't buy plastic bottles of water. Carry a water bottle with you. Use your bottle again and again.

You don't need a plastic straw with your drink. You can say, "No, thank you!"

Reduce! You don't want more plastic.
Choose things with no plastic at
the shops. Look at these two skateboards.
Which skateboard has more plastic?

Think before you buy new things.
You don't need a new plastic football.
You can play with your old football!

Reuse! We can use many old things again. Don't buy plastic bags at the shop. Take a shopping bag and reuse it.

These children are making toys. What are they using? They're using plastic bottles!

We can refuse, reduce or reuse plastic.
These are the best things to do.

But we can recycle some plastic, too.
We can recycle plastic bottles and
food boxes. Always clean plastic before
you recycle it.

What can we make with recycled plastic?
This car is recycled plastic. And this road
reuses old plastic, too!

Do we want mountains of plastic rubbish?
No, we don't.

Let's reduce our plastic rubbish today!
What ideas can you think of?

"Do you want a plastic water bottle, now?" asks Dad.

"No, thanks," says Matt. "Let's go home and get my water bottle."

"Good idea," says Dad.

Picture dictionary

Listen and repeat

plastic bottle

recycle

rubbish

shopping bag

straw

throw away

1 Look and say "Yes" or "No"

Fish sometimes eat plastic.

Plastic is good for fish.

There is no plastic in our seas.

Plastic rubbish is not good.

Some plastic in the sea is very old.

2 Listen and say

Collins

Published by Collins
An imprint of HarperCollins*Publishers*
Westerhill Road
Bishopbriggs
Glasgow
G64 2QT

HarperCollins*Publishers*
1st Floor, Watermarque Building
Ringsend Road
Dublin 4
Ireland

William Collins' dream of knowledge for all began with the publication of his first book in 1819.

A self-educated mill worker, he not only enriched millions of lives, but also founded a flourishing publishing house. Today, staying true to this spirit, Collins books are packed with inspiration, innovation and practical expertise. They place you at the centre of a world of possibility and give you exactly what you need to explore it.

© HarperCollins*Publishers* Limited 2020

10 9 8 7 6 5 4 3 2

ISBN 978-0-00-839682-4

Collins® and COBUILD® are registered trademarks of HarperCollins*Publishers* Limited

www.collins.co.uk/elt

British Library Cataloguing in Publication Data

A catalogue record for this publication is available from the British Library.

Author: Susannah Reed
Illustrator: Abdi (Beehive)
Series editor: Rebecca Adlard
Commissioning editor: Zoë Clarke
Publishing manager: Lisa Todd
Product managers: Jennifer Hall and Caroline Green
In-house editor: Alma Puts Keren
Project manager: Emily Hooton
Editor: Matthew Hancock
Proofreaders: Natalie Murray and Michael Lamb
Cover designer: Kevin Robbins
Typesetter: 2Hoots Publishing Services Ltd
Audio produced by id audio, London
Reading guide author: Emma Wilkinson
Production controller: Rachel Weaver
Printed and bound by: GPS Group, Slovenia

Download the audio for this book and a reading guide for parents and teachers at www.collins.co.uk/839682